SCHOLASTIC
Let's Find Out
My REBUS Reader

Let's Go to the Grocery Store

by Amanda Miller

SCHOLASTIC INC.
New York Toronto London Auckland Sydney New Delhi Hong Kong

We can buy  .

vegetables

We can buy .

fruit

We can buy  eggs and  milk.

We can buy  .

nuts

We can buy  .

bread

We can buy  .

cheese

Look at all our food! Yum!